INSURRECTION DAY
A GRAPHIC TIMELINE

The January 6th, 2021, Insurrection was based on a BIG LIE. A political lie is an attempt to trick a large group into believing something major, which will likely be contradicted by some information the group already possesses or by their common sense. When the lie is of sufficient magnitude it may succeed due to the group's reluctance to believe that an untruth on such a grand scale would indeed be concocted.

As we along with the majority of the country, watched in horror as the Insurrection unfolded, we were angry at the misinformation that created the BIG LIE. This deception helped lead to the attack of the Capitol that we all witnessed in real time. As of this publication, the Republican Party is still attempting to control the narrative and act as though January 6th was a peaceful protest.

This publication is a historical timeline of some of the events that led up to and became a coup attempt by the former president. The entire country was a witness to these events as they took place. This was a dark day for our democracy and a warning for the future of our republic.

"Democracy's a very fragile thing. You have to take care of democracy. As soon as you stop being responsible to it and allow it to turn into scare tactics, it's no longer democracy, is it? It's something else. It may be an inch away from totalitarianism."

~ Sam Shepard, Actor and Director

Benjamin Franklin was asked after the Constitutional Convention in 1787,
"Well, Doctor, what have we got, a republic or a monarchy?"
With no hesitation whatsoever, Franklin responded,
"A republic, if you can keep it."

CAN WE KEEP IT?

6th Sense Solutions
P.O. Box 17431
Seattle, WA 98127

Creative director & producer: Peter McKinnon

6th Sense Solutions is a creation of
Peter McKinnon and Jon deLeeuw

Content Consultant and Concerned Citizen: Jon deLeeuw

ISBN: 979-8-9855368-1-2

Website: 6thSenseSolutions.org

May we never be indifferent to
the events of January 6th, 2021.
The country, police forces
that protected our government,
and generations to come
deserve no less.

"Indifference, after all, is more
dangerous than anger and hatred."
"Indifference is not a beginning;
it is an end. And, therefore,
indifference is always the friend of
the enemy, for it benefits the
aggressor—never his victim,
whose pain is magnified when he
or she feels forgotten."

Elie Wiesel

6TH SENSE SOLUTIONS OPINION

The opinion of this publication is to establish the premise that the events leading up to and on January 6th, 2021, were fabricated on the "BIG LIE" told by Trump and his associates. The nation observed and saw the results of the election not favoring Trump. Trump lost but did not concede the results as he should have humbly done. Instead he rallied the Republican party and cult-like followers and lied to them. The way this country has always worked, is by the peaceful transfer of power when the public votes a president and his party out of office.

By the popular vote, Trump was not the majority choice in 2016. Opposition voters against Trump watched helplessly as he continued to dismantle norms as a president. His incompetence during the Covid-19 crisis ultimately led to excess deaths of hundreds of thousands of Americans. Trump had clear guidance on procedures and recommendations from our top doctors and scientists, and yet he was 'smarter than them all'. In fact, he influenced people to distrust medical and scientific common sense, to the point of advocating drinking bleach to cure Covid-19.

When Trump rode the escalator down in 2015, many people felt no one in their right mind would ever vote for a conman and reality TV Show Host like Trump.

Much to our shock we found out there are a lot of Americans willing to be conned (unfortunately these were the people who showed up on January 6th). Although Hillary Clinton won by the popular vote, due to the electoral college Trump was declared president-elect.

Before and after Trump was elected in 2016, he continued to sow distrust in our election process. The continuous social media assault by our former president on our normal democratic processes led to fertile soil for the growth of the BIG LIE.

Elle Wiesel, a Jewish author, philosopher and human-ist made it his life's work to bear witness to the geno-cide committed by the Nazis during World War II, says **"We must take sides. Neutrality helps the oppressor, never the victim. Silence encourages the tormentor, never the tormented. Sometimes we must interfere. When human lives are endangered, when human dig-nity is in jeopardy, national borders and sensitivities become irrelevant. Wherever men and women are persecuted because of their race, religion, or politi-cal views, that place must - at that moment - become the center of the universe."**

THE DERANGED ASPECTS OF TRUMP

Excerpts from the Psychology Today article,
The Psychology of Trump,
by Darcia F. Narvaez Ph.D.

In 2017, a group of mental health professionals gathered at a "duty to warn" conference and then published their informed opinions in the book, *The Dangerous Case of Trump*, contending that he was unfit to be president (Lee, 2017). In the book, they illustrated their professional perceptions of Trump (DT) with his statements and actions known to that point. (See also the 2020 film, *Unfit*, for more discussions of the psychology of DT by clinicians.)

Many of the mental health professionals drew a connection between Trump's behavior and extreme or pathological narcissism (narcissistic personality disorder) which entails entitlement, exploitation, and empathy impairment, along with the typical characteristics of narcissism:

- Believing you are superior to others
- Fantasizing about success
- Exaggerating talents and achievements
- Expecting constant admiration and praise
- Believing you are special and acting that way
- Failing to recognize others' feelings
- Expecting others to do what you want
- Taking advantage of others
- Expressing disdain for the "inferior"
- Jealousy of others
- Easily hurt and rejected
- Having a fragile self-esteem

- Appearing tough and unemotional
- Setting unrealistic goals
- Unable to keep healthy relationships

Lance Dodes, M.D., reminded readers of the characteristics of antisocial personality disorder:

- Failure to conform to laws and social norms
- Deceitfulness
- Impulsive
- Irritability and aggressiveness
- Reckless disregard for safety of others and of self
- Pattern of irresponsibility
- Lack of remorse
- Conduct disorder (impulsive, aggressiveness, callousness, and deceitfulness starting before age 15)

Read more here: Psychology Today Article

This ain't America for you and me

Violently storming the Capitol is not patriotic. This is not what we are all about; this is like children throwing a tantrum because they are not getting their way. It's disgraceful, and it could have been avoided with two simple words, "I concede" by the person who lost the election to now president Joe Biden by 7 million plus votes. Everyone in this country saw the results; it went to Biden.

Biden is our president, and no one is going to break the laws of the United States of America to change our election results.

TIMELINE TO INSURRECTION

2020

NOV. 3: ELECTION NIGHT
Trump falsely claims victory: "We were getting ready to win this election. Frankly, we did win this election."

NOV. 7: BIDEN WINS
News networks accurately report that Joe Biden had won the election. Rather than concede and acknowledge the result, Trump's allies launched dozens of baseless lawsuits.

NOV. 9: TRUMP REFUSES TO CONCEDE
Relentlessly, Trump attacks the election as *"rigged"* and *"stolen."* Trump and his allies then lose more than 60 lawsuits, focusing on all the swing states. *"Stop the Steal"* becomes a rallying cry. To this day, Trump has not conceded.

DEC. 19: PROMOTING JANUARY 6TH
Trump tweets about the January 6th gathering to protest the Electoral College win for Biden. *"Big protests in D.C. on January 6. Be there. Will be wild!"* It was one of several times he promoted the rally.

2021

JAN. 3: DOJ INVOLVEMENT
Trump considers replacing Rosen with a lower-ranking department official, Jeffrey Clark, who was promising to pursue Trump's false election fraud claims. Rosen and his deputies refused to endorse Trump's claims, and pushed back against the president's proposed scheme to dump Rosen for Clark.

JAN. 3: POLICE WARNED
An internal Capitol Police intelligence report warns that enraged protesters, flanked by white supremacists and extreme militia groups, are likely to arrive in Washington armed for battle and target Congress on January 6.

JAN. 4: LEADING UP TO ATTACK
Trump tells a Georgia rally, *"Together we are taking back our country. We will not bend, we will not break, we will not yield. We will never give in, we will never give up, we will never back down. We will never, ever surrender."* Words like these are repeated at the January 6th rally.

JANUARY 6TH, 2021: ATTACK ON CAPITOL
As Congress began formally counting the Electoral College votes, the president, his lawyer, and other allies addressed a crowd that included Proud Boys, assorted extremist groups and numerous people wearing QAnon paraphernalia. *"Let's have a trial by combat!"* Giuliani proclaimed. *"You'll never take back our country with weakness,"* Trump said. *"You have to show strength and you have to be strong."* Trump incites the crowd that he had been priming with lies, and sent them to disrupt and stop the Congressional proceedings.

Also see: Timeline of the 2021 United States Capitol attack

6thsenseSolutions.org

Thousands of people gathered on January 6th, 2021 to fight against what they were deceived to believe was a stolen election. To the majority of us, the election was fair and checked thoroughly by the Trump administration.

JANUARY 6TH, 2021 RADIO BROADCAST

By Peter McKinnon

On January 6th, I was at the hospital going through a medical procedure around mid-morning Pacific time. When I left the hospital, I decided to get coffee on the way home. As I was driving, I turned on NPR and was taken by surprise at what I thought was a "War of the Worlds" type broadcast. The Insurrection attack was happening in real time. There was chaos and mayhem as an attack on our seat of power and sacred United States Capitol was being besieged. I went home and like many other Americans, glued myself to the TV News for the rest of the day.

It seemed crazy to me at the time that people would be violently protesting a fair election. Biden had clearly won, more so than Bush W. in 2000 and Trump in 2016. Biden won by millions in the popular vote and clearly won the electoral college, as well. So why were these people marching? I found out they'd been lied to over-and-over again by the person they loved and respected, and he took advantage of their trust.

We now call this the "BIG LIE", although it is much more than just a lie; it's a betrayal of our constitution, our government, our institutions, and our basic principles of fair play. It's a method of deception we have not had to face on such a public level before; it's treason to our laws and American way of life. All this is true, and at the same time we are living with a governing body that seems too fearful of putting Trump on trial for his actions. Because of this, Trump continues the "BIG LIE".

I am older and can remember when Bill Clinton was put on trial for something far less serious to our country than a coup. What has happened to our justice department, our FBI, and our prosecutors who seem to be waiting for more harm to fall on our country? As of this writing, Trump is free from being accountable for his illegal activities.

It all started before the election in 2016 when Trump announced that if he didn't win the election it was rigged. That was the beginning of a Pandora's box of lies and complete deception of the truth. For four years of his presidency, we never got a day of rest from the narcissistic tweets of an insecure president. Trump has lied so much that everyone seems to be numb from the onslaught of Trump's continued deception since taking the POTUS stage. To this day, we don't know the full truth about Trump's loyalty to Putin and how the Russians really did tamper with the 2016 election results. We also don't know why Trump's taxes were not an issue in 2016 but have revealed a background of corruption within his own organization to hide funds and taxes due. It makes me wonder, how much more could Trump have done to get to where he could be running for office at all.

The purpose of this publication is to highlight the absurdities of January 6th. I have studied many articles and gathered a number of images and made them into a graphic editorial to show the events before, during and after the Insurrection. My concern is indifference and complacency to the event of January 6th, 2021. Those involved should not be ignored like spoiled children acting out their anger and aggression by bullying. Far more than bullying, this was violence that resulted in deaths. As the Dude says, in "The Big Lebowski", "This will not stand, ya know, this aggression will not stand, man."

Even as of October 2021, Trump claimed after learning that he lost by more votes in Arizona than previously counted by Cyber Ninja's, that he won. It appears idiotic to most Americans, that people would still be putting up with Trump's level of false information. Nothing seems to get through to the cult followers of Trump. His sheep would run off a cliff for him.

One of the worst aspects of January 6th, 2021 was pointed out by my friend that day on Facebook, who resides on the other side of the planet in Sydney Australia. He said that if the protesters were black and protesting BLM while entering the Capitol, they'd all be dead. **The world was watching and coming up with that same conclusion that day.**

FALSE CLAIMS BUILD UP TO INSURRECTION

November 7, 2020, four days after the United States presidential election, Rudy Giuliani, the attorney for then-president Trump, hosted a press conference. It was held (to the delight of many a comedian since then) at Four Seasons Total Landscaping, a small business adjacent to a sex-toy emporium near Philadelphia, Pennsylvania. It garnered further ridicule after it emerged that one of the speakers at the event was a convicted sex offender.

"Woodward and Costa have Trump telling advisers that, yes, Giuliani is 'crazy,' but 'none of the sane lawyers can represent me because they've been pressured.'

Lee Holmes, chief counsel for the Trump supporter Senator Lindsey Graham, is portrayed in "Peril" as 'astonished at the overreach' of fraud claims by Giuliani and others. Holmes wrote to Graham that the data behind the claims were 'a concoction, with a bullying tone and eighth-grade writing.' (Graham disagreed. 'Third grade,' he said.)"

Source: New York Times
book review of *Peril*,
by John Williams, Sept. 17, 2021

Legal Team BIG LIE Meltdown After The Election

In November of 2020, Giuliani asked "Did you all watch 'My Cousin Vinny?' You know, the movie?". He was sweating at a lectern in the small lobby of the Republican National Committee headquarters on Capitol Hill. "It's one of my favorite law movies, 'cause he comes from Brooklyn."

 "How many finguhs do I got up?" Giuliani said at the lectern, doing a terrible Joe Pesci, from the scene where he cross-examines an elderly eyewitness with bad eyesight. Giuliani was trying to analogize the claims of Republican poll watchers, who say they were too far away from ballot counting to adequately observe it. Fifteen minutes later, as he was making his own false statement that the election results were "a massive fraud," black liquid began to slowly streak from each of his temples, down his cheeks.

If Rudy is deteriorating, then so is the audience that listens to him and who want to believe him. For 90 minutes, an unmasked Rudy and four maskless colleagues — "an elite strike force team," according to senior legal adviser Jenna Ellis — spun a ridiculous web of conspiracies that indicate Trump won the election that he lost. A revolution, they said, was at hand.

"It is the 1775 of our generation," declared fellow strike force team member Sidney Powell, who once appeared on Fox Business to claim that an immigrant "invasion" is spreading "polio-like paralysis" among American children. She continued: "Globalists, dictators, corporations, you name it — everybody's against us except President Trump."

Excerpts from "*Rudy Giuliani's post-election meltdown starts to become literal*", Washington Post, By Dan Zak and Josh Dawsey, November 19, 2020

The gas-lighting legal strategy of President Donald J. Trump's lawyers of trying to convince the public of the BIG LIE worked. His MAGA followers believed it was true. Giuliani fictionalized votes that could've been cast by dead people, Mickey Mouse, Chinese hackers, Vikings, Frosty the snow man, space lasers, Bozo the clown or what ever make believe actors he could come up with. It was all a lie, and most of us know that, except the people who showed up on January 6th to disrupt congress.

The "Kraken" cases: coming up from the depths with false claims established by Trump's lawyers

A federal judge in Michigan had ordered that Sidney Powell, L. Lin Wood and seven other attorneys who filed a lawsuit seeking to overturn the state's 2020 presidential election be disciplined, calling the suit "a historic and profound abuse of the judicial process." [1]

U.S. District Judge Linda V. Parker said she would rule on a request to discipline the lawyers in coming weeks. But over and over again during the more than five-hour hearing, she pointedly pressed the lawyers involved — including Trump allies Sidney Powell and L. Lin Wood — to explain what steps they had taken to ensure their court filings in the case filed last year had been accurate. She appeared astonished by many of their answers. [2]

A federal judge granted the motion of sanctions filed by the state of Michigan and the city of Detroit against the so-called "Kraken" attorneys over their conspiracy-tinged litigation hoping to overturn the 2020 presidential election, ordering that they face "possible suspension or disbarment" and be referred for a professional conduct probe.

"This lawsuit represents a historic and profound abuse of the judicial process," Parker wrote in a lengthy 110-page ruling. "It is one thing to take on the charge of vindicating rights associated with an allegedly fraudulent election. It is another to take on the charge of deceiving a federal court and the American people into believing that rights were infringed, without regard to whether any laws or rights were in fact violated. This is what happened here." [3]

The Kraken cases argued that Biden's win had been marred by fraud and asked Parker to require that Trump instead be declared the winner of Michigan's 16 electoral votes. Parker rejected the request in

Giuliani's witness, Melissa Carone, draws audible laughter during her unfounded testimony. Later this made for a great SNL sketch.

December, writing that she was being asked to disenfranchise "more than 5.5 million Michigan citizens who, with dignity, hope, and a promise of a voice, participated in the 2020 General Election."

She added that the plaintiffs had advanced "nothing but speculation and conjecture that votes for President Trump were destroyed, discarded or switched to votes for Vice President Biden."

Lawyers for the city of Detroit, as well as Attorney General Dana Nessel (D), acting on behalf of the state's governor and secretary of state, had moved for the lawyers to be disciplined.

"It has remained abundantly clear from the outset that this lawsuit aimed to do nothing more than undermine our democratic process," Nessel said in a statement. "I appreciated Judge Parker's thorough-

ness in the hearing last month, and I appreciate the unmistakable message she sends with this ruling — those who vow to uphold the Constitution must answer for abandoning that oath." [1]

[1] "Federal judge in Michigan orders pro-Trump lawyers disciplined over lawsuit seeking to overturn 2020 election" by Rosalind Helderman of the Washington Post

[2] "This is really fantastical': Federal judge in Michigan presses Trump-allied lawyers on 2020 election fraud claims in sanctions hearing" by Rosalind Helderman of the Washington Post

[3] "Judge Sanctions Pro-Trump 'Kraken' Lawyers for 'Debasing' Courts With Bogus Election Lawsuits" by Justin Baragona
Media Reporter for the Daily Beast

Like his fascist predecessor, Trump thought that he could amass a group of Insurrectionists and take over the government. The Declaration of Independence though, desired a strong democracy against dictator take overs. That is why our country kicked out King George III of England in 1776.

On January 6th, 2021, Trump directed the people he deceived, causing them to become Insurrectionists, by pointing them toward the Capitol building and telling them to fight like hell to steal the election for him. He gave a speech flanked by his kids, Rudy Giuliani, and other unsavory characters. He tried to gather as many people around him as he could into his crime.

The country watched in horror and disgust as Trump tried to steal an election in front of the whole world. So the siege of the Capitol began, after 6 weeks of preparation with GOP senators and congress members undergoing covert actions to direct the Insurrectionists into the building. It was a Trump coup in the making from the start.

The BIG LIE was in full swing now, and all that was left was a march on the Capitol to attack our democracy. From the perspective of these marchers, Trump told them he won, and they fully believed him (there is no secret he's a conman, liar and cheater). It was what he taught them to do. Now they are co-conspirators with Trump as the leader.

   INSURRECTION DAY   JANUARY 6TH, 2021

The BIG LIE was now burning bright like a forest fire, burning all the truth in it's wake; flags flying, signs made about "Stop the Treason" (the lie), people angry and some with automatic rifles in hand. It was all played live on our TV sets, radios and by the press from around the world. It was a coup staged on our fair election process, and some within the Congress and Senate were in on the sedition by rejecting that process and fueling the flame of this Insurrection. Holding American flags like they were at a Nazi Third Reich convention, people were not patriotic; they were neurotic for a lie that was spun by the leader they love. We are talking about a pussy grabbing, tax evading, bankrupt, draft dodger, who is a conman from New York City. It's hard to believe people like this guy. Trump turned these people from being Americans to Terrorists. The pictures don't lie, but Trump sure does.

"Hang Mike Pence!", "Hang Mike Pence!", "Hang Mike Pence!", "Hang Mike Pence!", "Hang Mike Pence!", was broadcast live to a horrified (or maybe terrified) world. The coup was bent on killing our Vice President because he was doing his job as VP. Our government had to run and hide that day from being destroyed. The mob had military gear on, and were stocked full of paramilitary personnel. A terrorist group encroached upon our Capitol steps and smashed their way into the building.

    INSURRECTION DAY   JANUARY 6TH, 2021

Ulysses S. Grant predicted that the next civil war would be "between patriotism and intelligence on one side, and superstition, ambition, and ignorance on the other."

Words to know and understand about what happened on January 6th, 2021:

Sedition

noun

Incitement of resistance to or Insurrection against lawful authority

Examples of sedition in a sentence: The leaders of the group have been arrested and charged with sedition.

Insurrection

Noun

A usually violent attempt to take control of a government

He led an armed Insurrection [rebellion, uprising] against the elected government.

Acts of Insurrection

Full Definition of Insurrection: An act or instance of revolting against civil authority or an established government.

To be clear, what happened on January 6th, 2021 was an armed Insurrection. Clearly Trump committed treason that day by inciting his mob to violence against our Congress. People were climbing walls, breaking windows, and entering our Capitol to commit crimes against our country. They turned from being self-described patriots to terrorists in the walk from the White House to our Capitol. Crossing that line, they became traitors to all our branches of government and our military services.

Officers fight for their lives as an angry mob based on
false information attacks our elected government in
a coup effort to change the results in favor of Trump.
It's been noted that this is the most photographed and
videoed incident in history.

The majority of our country was in shock to see so
many people under Trump's spell. Trump used the term
"witch-hunt" about everything leveled against him.
Maybe we can now say he has a witch like spell over
people, so witch-hunt fits.

The attack on the Capitol really benefited enemies of democracy by undermining our peaceful transition of power and the processes we have established for a couple of hundred years. Putin's investment in Trump has paid off. China also benefits from seeing our weakness. It's as if Putin lent the ladder to step things up.

Who brings ladders to a peaceful protest?

It was frightening to see our congressional representatives in this situation of fearing for their lives. Insurrectionists broke in and disrupted the procedures of the day, looking through paperwork and acting as if it was a normal day for them to commit crimes against our nation.

A now familiar face, which I call buffalo man (the Q-anon Shaman). QAnon is known to be one of the conspiracies containing the most false information out there. Buffalo man is just another person under a spell (later to be sentenced to four years in prison).

Look! Here's another Insurrectionist stealing from our halls of congress. Thankfully there were folks outside saying "stop the steal". If only they meant not stealing Nancy Pelosi's podium.

It's sad to see the flag of traitors within the halls of congress. It makes a statement that these aren't Americans attacking our country when they have a flag with a repulsive history.

Legal experts say a wide variety of crimes occurred, and prosecutors could charge individuals even if they walked away from the incident without being detained. Members of the mob could be charged with trespassing, the "willful injury of federal property," and firearms offenses. Two explosive devices were recovered. A specific statute governs unlawful activities on the grounds of the U.S. Capitol, making it illegal to "step or climb on, remove, or in any way injure any statue, seat, wall, fountain, or other erection or architectural feature, or any tree, shrub, plant, or turf."

There's a ton of evidence available to prosecutors, including forensic proof such as fingerprints. Much of the criminal activity took place on live television, providing ample footage that can be combined with facial-recognition technology to identify suspects. Legal experts say it's likely that even before the mayhem unfolded, undercover investigators were prowling social media to monitor whoever was organizing it. Suspects may have postings that provide evidence of their intent.

Source: "How Might the U.S. Capitol Rioters Face Justice?" By Erik Larson and Joel Rosenblatt, Bloomberg, January 6, 2021

Update as of this publication's date many members of the mob have been charged in federal court.

Shocking headlines from the media followed the January 6th, 2021 events. Words like Insurrection, attack, assault, stormed and siege were common in phrases used about that day.

Conspiracy

Noun

A secret plan by a group to do something unlawful or harmful.

The Insurrection was a conspiracy by Trump to overturn our election.

All the above newspapers' headlines highlight this fact.

HOUSE & SENATE MEMBERS AGAINST THE ELECTION

Lauren Boebert, Colo.

Ron Johnson, Wis.

Marjorie Taylor Greene, GA

Paul Gosar, Ariz.

Elise M. Stefanik, N.Y.

Josh Hawley, Mo.

"Even after a mob of Trump support-ers swarmed and entered the Capitol on Wednesday, a handful of Republican senators and more than 100 Republican representatives stood by their decisions to vote against certifying the results of the presidential election."

Source: *"Here are the Republicans who objected to certifying the election results."* By Jenny Gross and Luke Broadwater, New York Times, Jan. 8, 2021

SENATE

Tommy Tuberville, AL

Rick Scott, FL

Roger Marshall, KS

John Kennedy, LA

Cindy Hyde-Smith, MS

Josh Hawley, MO

Ted Cruz, TX

Cynthia Lummis, WY

CONGRESS

Robert B. Aderholt, AL

Mo Brooks, AL

Jerry Carl, AL

Barry Moore, AL

Gary Palmer, AL

Mike Rogers, AL

Andy Biggs, AR

Paul Gosar, AZ

Debbie Lesko, AZ

David   , AZ

Rick Crawford, AR

Ken Calvert, CA

Mike Garcia, CA

Darrell   , CA

Doug LaMalfa, CA

Kevin McCarthy, CA

Devin Nunes, CA

Jay Obernolte, CA

Lauren Boebert, CO

Doug Lamborn, CO

Kat Cammack, FL

Mario Diaz-Balart, FL

Byron Donalds, FL

Neal Dunn, FL

Scott Franklin, FL

Matt Gaetz, FL

Carlos Gimenez, FL

Brian Mast, FL

Bill Posey, FL

John Rutherford, FL

Greg Steube, FL

Daniel Webster, FL

Rick Allen, GA

Earl L. "Buddy" Carter, GA

Andrew Clyde, GA

Marjorie Taylor Greene, GA

Jody Hice, GA

Barry Loudermilk, GA

Russ Fulcher, ID

Mike Bost, IL

Mary Miller, IL

Jim Baird, IN

Jim Banks, IN

Greg Pence, IN

Jackie Walorski, IN

Ron Estes, KS

Jacob LaTurner, KS

Tracey Mann, KS

Harold Rogers, KY

Garret Graves, LA

Clay Higgins, LA

Mike Johnson, LA

Steve Scalise, LA

Andy Harris, MD

Jack Bergman, MI

Lisa McClain, MI

Tim Walberg, MI

Michelle Fischbach, MN

Jim Hagedorn, MN

Michael Guest, MS

Trent Kelly, MS.

Steven Palazzo, MS

Sam Graves, MO

Vicky Hartzler, MO

Billy Long, MO

Blaine Luetkemeyer, MO

Jason Smith, MO

Matt Rosendale, MT

Dan Bishop, NC

Ted Budd, NC

Madison Cawthorn, NC

Virginia Foxx, NC

Richard Hudson, NC

Gregory F. Murphy, NC

David Rouzer, NC

Jeff Van Drew, NJ

Yvette Herrell, NM

Chris Jacobs, NY

Nicole Malliotakis, NY

Elise M. Stefanik, NY

Lee Zeldin, NY

Adrian Smith, NE

Steve Chabot, OH

Warren Davidson, OH

Bob Gibbs, OH

Bill Johnson, OH

Jim Jordan, OH

Stephanie Bice, OK

Tom Cole, OK

Kevin Hern, OK

Frank Lucas, OK

Markwayne Mullin, OK

Cliff Bentz, OR

John Joyce, PA

Fred Keller, PA

Mike Kelly, PA

Daniel Meuser, PA

Scott Perry, PA

Guy Reschenthaler, PA

Lloyd Smucker, PA

Glenn Thompson, PA

Jeff Duncan, SC

Ralph Norman, SC

Tom Rice, SC

William Timmons, SC

Joe Wilson, SC

Tim Burchett, TN

Scott DesJarlais, TN

Chuck Fleischmann, TN

Mark E. Green, TN

Diana Harshbarger, TN

David Kustoff, TN

John Rose, TN

Jodey Arrington, TX

Brian Babin, TX

Michael C. Burgess, TX

John R. Carter, TX

Michael Cloud, TX

Pat Fallon, TX

Louie Gohmert, TX

Lance Gooden, TX

Ronny Jackson, TX

Troy Nehls, TX

August Pfluger, TX

Pete Sessions, TX

Beth Van Duyne, TX

Randy Weber, TX

Roger Williams, TX

Ron Wright, TX

Burgess Owens, UT

Chris Stewart, UT

Ben Cline, VA

Bob Good, VA

Morgan Griffith, VA

Robert J. Wittman, VA

Carol Miller, WV

Alexander X. Mooney, WV

Scott Fitzgerald, WI

Tom Tiffany, WI

In the next election, remember these members of our government who voted against our democracy and vote them all out of office. They betrayed their oath of office.

Vote these traitors out of office!

Not one of these members of Congress and the Senate is truthful in their actions post January 6th, 2021. They are a disgrace to their oath of office to defend the constitution of the United States.

Definition of a lie

"A lie is an assertion that is believed to be false, typically used with the purpose of deceiving someone. The practice of communicating lies is called lying. A person who communicates a lie may be termed a liar. Lies may serve a variety of instrumental, interpersonal, or psychological functions for the individuals who use them.

Generally, the term "lie" carries a negative connotation, and depending on the context a person who communicates a lie may be subject to social, legal, religious, or criminal sanctions."

Wikipedia

Mo Brooks, AL, stood at the podium with Trump on January 6th, and has been suspected as one of the insiders that worked with January 6th Insurrectionist planners.

Lauren Boebert, has been suspected as one of the insiders that worked with planners of the January 6th attack.

Marjorie Taylor Greene has been suspected of being one of the insiders that worked with planners of the January 6th attack. Note the message on her mask.

Jim Jordan, OH and Matt Gaetz, FL voted against certification of Biden as President.

Insiders Revealed

According to Vice News, two sources from the planning group of the January 6th attack, say they were in direct and regular contact with Republican Reps. Marjorie Taylor Greene of Georgia, Mo Brooks of Alabama, Madison Cawthorn of North Carolina, Louie Gohmert of Texas, and Lauren Boebert of Colorado—fierce Trump allies who have since the January 6 riots downplayed their violence while complaining about the treatment of those who've been arrested for committing crimes that day. The sources also say former White House Chief of Staff Mark Meadows, a former House Freedom Caucus member, was deeply involved as well.

Treason

Treason is the crime of attacking a state authority to which one owes allegiance. This typically includes acts such as participating in a war against one's native country, attempting to overthrow its government, spying on its military, its diplomats, or its secret services for a hostile and foreign power, or attempting to kill its head of state. A person who commits treason is known in law as a traitor.

Wikipedia

Definition of Traitor

A person who betrays a friend, country, principle, etc.

Wikipedia

The GOP is now known as the anti-democracy party

"Anybody fighting Joe Biden is helping Trump's next coup" said Jonathon Chiat in NYMag.com. Republicans in the House and Senate are continuing to kiss Trump's ring in loyalty to his ascension as the head of the now Trump party (the old GOP). The GOP party has continued the talk about corrupting the election process by throwing out Democratic votes within big cities. This is the authoritarian threat of our lifetime within our own borders of the United States of America. Hitler, Stalin and Mao took total control within their perspective countries; the Republicans are trying to do the same in our country. To many of us, January 6th looks like the beginning of something even worse if we don't convict the people in charge of allowing it to happen before the next election in 2024.

As of this publication's date the Oath Keepers leader and 10 others charged with 'seditious conspiracy' related to US Capitol attack

TRUMP THE GRIFTER AND CONMAN

We've all seen it for our entire lives. Trump is a deal maker. He's even sold out his own brother to gain more favor with his father, as told in Mary Trump's book, "Too Much and Never Enough: How My Family Created the World's Most Dangerous Man". So it is no surprise that in the end he sold out for political power.

The big lesson about Trump is the exposure he has brought to many of the corrupt dealings of our government with him being smack dab in the middle of how easy it is to swindle the American people. He's over charged the government on the use of his own properties to make deals with foreign powers

that are not in the best interest of our country (i.e.- his deal with the Taliban before he left office). Now he is on a rampage to bilk his followers of money from telling them the BIG LIE that he didn't lose in November of 2020.

As stated in the article "Follow the money: Understanding the deep roots of Trump's coup attempt" by Chauncey DeVega August 10th, 2021 in Salon, "The examples are legion: Trump was elected with the help of a hostile foreign power and appeared to do its leader's bidding throughout his presidency. Trump engaged in acts of democide against the American people through sabotage and willful neglect in response to the coronavirus pandemic."

Another article of interest to sum things up is from Heather Cox Richardson's "Letters from an American" on October 31, 2021 where she says: "And here we are, and yes it is.

Washington Post published a long report about the events before, during, and after January 6, compiled by a team of more than 25 reporters and additional staff who reviewed video and court transcripts, followed social media posts, and interviewed more than 230 people. The report lays the blame for January 6 on Trump and warns that we are in a fight for the survival of democracy."

Richardson also says that the report concluded: "Trump was the driving force at every turn as he orchestrated what would become an attempted political coup in the months leading up to Jan. 6, calling his supporters to Washington, encouraging the mob to march on the Capitol and freezing in place key federal agencies whose job it was to investigate and stop threats to national security."

AFTERMATH

By Jon deLeeuw

As of this writing the events that led up to that day are still being made public. This book documents many of those that are publicly known, and shows in graphic detail the attack on the Capital. The right wing media is still portraying January 6th as Antifa caused, or even that day in the Capital was like any open visitors day. Emerging information makes clear that the "unplanned" riot on January 6th was very much pre-planned, instigated, and potentially aided by government officials at the highest levels including the ex-president. Yet, despite all this, the ex-president remains popular among the right, wielding tremendous power in the Republican Party. And Red states are doing their best to enact laws that disenfranchise voters.

One of the first things that can be done to contact or call elected representatives. It's easy to send an email or text, thousands of people sign petitions with the click of a button. A call takes time and means you are committed to the reason you are calling. Tell Senators to support HR1, the House bill supporting voting rights. Most especially contact Joe Manchin of West Virginia, and Kyrsten Sinema of Arizona, the two democratic senators standing in the way of passing HR 1. Find your elected representatives at USA.gov.

The second thing to tell Senators is support the work of the January 6th Commission. Encourage them to finish their work and send criminal referrals to the Department of Justice before the next election. The foot soldiers who physically participated in the Insurrection are currently being indicted and sentenced yet those who planned the Insurrection remain unaccountable. The Insurrectionist now know the weaknesses in the system. If no action is taken now, there's a good chance the next time they will succeed! Support candidates in the next election who support finishing the Commission's work.

On a local level, stay informed and active. Run for local office, attend school board meetings and city council meetings. Challenge misinformation when you encounter it. Make sure your local voting boards are not staffed by partisan officials. Get involved in talking and listening to people with opposing views. Concentrate on common ground rather than divisions. Check out TransPartisan.quest to get involved and learn techniques to help us all come to a place of healing and togetherness rather than fear and divisiveness.

> # "The next chapter of the Insurrection Saga is up to us"
> - Jon deLeeuw

"Those who vote decide nothing. Those who count the vote decide everything."

- Joseph Stalin, Former ruler of the Soviet Union responsible for 20 million deaths

"The world is run by those who show up"

- Robert Johnson, Musician and Songwriter

The creators of 6th Sense Solutions live in Washington state and love its mail in voting system. Neither has waited in a line to vote in years. They track their votes online and can ensure they were counted. And, if one doesn't trust the mail, one can drop it in any of the many available drop boxes. Plus, no worries about mail delays, because it will be counted as long as it is postmarked on or before election day. This system of voting is supported by a majority of Washington state citizens, yet even Washington State have congressional representatives supporting a return to our old system of voting. All US citizens should have the ease to vote which we have in Washington State, and the local representatives who don't support that should be voted out.

All US citizens should have the ease to vote which we have in Washington State, and the local representatives who don't support that should be voted out.

January 6th reminds
us of the Terrorists
Attack of 9/11 and
about how we'll never
forget where we were
and how it made
us feel.

The seriousness of
January 6th is like that
and worse because
we don't remember a
number of Americans
rooting for the
Terrorists.